The UNSOLVED MYSTERIES Project Book

Steve Barlow and Steve Skidmore
Illustrator Andrew Warrington

CONTENTS

BROCKHAMPTON PRESS
LONDON

Ghosts

What happens to us when we die? It may be that ghosts hold a clue to this mystery.

There are several theories to explain the appearance of ghosts:

- some may be unhappy spirits, seeking in death to put right the wrongs they did in life
- others are said to haunt the people responsible for their deaths
- some are reported to have given warning of approaching disasters.

Most ghosts seem simply to wish to be left alone. **Arthur Grimble**, a British diplomat stationed in the Gilbert Islands in the Pacific during the First World War, was offended when an old man brushed past him without speaking. He complained about the man's behaviour to the policeman who was walking with him, but his companion had not seen the man. When he reached his destination, Grimble was told that one of the villagers had died that afternoon and that he had seen the spirit of the man on its way to the Gate of the Dead.

Everybody has heard ghost stories, but do such beings actually exist?

In 1799 the ghost of a young girl once jilted by **Lord Thomas Lyttleton** appeared to him with the news that he had exactly three days to live. His friends reset the clocks in his house and the predicted hour seemed to pass without disaster. However, when the church clock later struck the true hour, the wicked Lord fell dead.

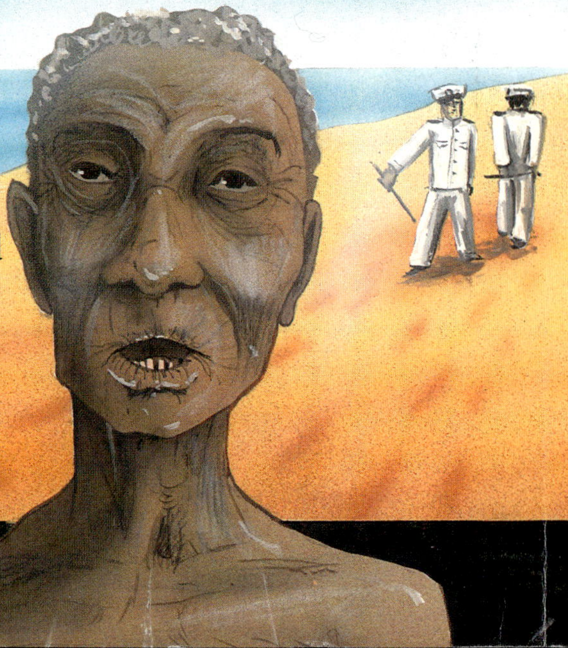

Poltergeists

Other ghosts move objects about, or smash them, and occasionally attack people. In 1716, one of these troublesome spirits visited the house of the Wesley family in England. **Old Jeffrey** bounced dishes, lifted doorlatches, and pushed people. We know about this spirit from the writings of the young John Wesley, who later became the founder of Primitive Methodism.

Old Jeffrey acted as a playmate for the younger Wesley children – but most poltergeists are more violent and dangerous. In Stratford, Connecticut in 1850, the Phelps family found eleven ghostly figures dressed in the family's clothes kneeling before bibles. For eighteen months, messages appeared, objects were thrown about and two of the older children were discovered at the point of death from attacks that afterwards they could not explain or remember.

Communication with spirits

Some ghosts are transparent, others seem able to take on solid forms. Attempts to contact spirits were popular in Victorian England. **Mediums**, who claimed to be able to make contact with the spirit world, held **seances** to try to contact the spirits of the dead. Some mediums were fakes, but others may well have been genuine.

The saddest and most desperate attempt to contact spirits was probably that made by the **Sioux Ghost Dancers**. They were told by the prophet Wovoka that he could teach them a dance that would raise up the ghosts of their ancestors, sweep away the white men and return the buffalo and the horses to the plains.

As the Ghost Dancers gathered at Wounded Knee, the US Army responded by attacking and killing 300 out of the 350 men, women and children present.

Haunted houses

One of the most famous haunted houses is **Glamis Castle** in Scotland, which is said to have at least nine ghosts, including that of **Macbeth**, the murderous Thane of Shakespeare's play. It is also said that a hidden room in the castle contains a dreadful secret, known only to the Earls of Glamis, and as one of them considered the story too horrifying to pass on to his son, the truth may never be known.

Some right royal spooks

Catherine Howard**, Henry VIII's fifth wife, ibout to be beheaded, begged in vain for nercy. Her shrieks can still be heard in the ong gallery at Hampton Court.

Anne Boleyn, and **ane Seymour**, two more of Henry's queens, ılso haunt Hampton Court.

While **Henry VIII** himself eems to haunt Windsor Castle along with **Queen Elizabeth I** nd the poor mad vraith of **George III.**

Visitors to the Tower of London have even reported seeing the ghost of a **bear**, once kept in the Tower zoo.

The most grisly ghost to haunt the Tower of London is the **Countess of Salisbury**, who 1 1541 refused to kneel at the block, but an screaming in terror round the scaffold while the executioner chased her vith his axe.

Amazing haunting facts

The most haunted house in England was **Borley Rectory** in Essex.

- From 1863 to 1939, more than 200 sightings were reported.
- The most sighted Borley ghost was a nun called **Marie Lairre** who was murdered in 1667.
- When the house burned down in 1939, onlookers saw strange figures in the flames, including one in the form of a nun.
- Four years later, the bones of a young woman were found beneath the cellar floor . . .

UFOs

Throughout history there have been reports of mysterious objects in the sky from all around the world.

'UFO' follow
US pla

Many of these sightings can be logically explained, but there are some reports that defy reasonable explanation.

Do these Unidentified Flying Objects (UFOs) exist only in people's imaginations? Are they top secret military aircraft, or are they spacecraft built and flown by creatures from other planets? There are many theories about UFOs, but as far as the general public are concerned, UFOs remain a mystery.

This 'UFO' is in f
a bu

Official modern investigations into UFOs only began in 1933 after sightings of *ghost aircraft* were reported in Scandinavia, Britain and the US. Since then, there have been thousands of reports of UFOs from all around the world. Sometimes there have been photographs to support these claims, but unfortunately, as many of them have been faked, people are sceptical about all photographic evidence.

A faked photograph?

On 28 March 1966 at about 8.30pm, Stephen Pratt and his mother saw a throbbing light in the sky near their home in Conisbrough, Yorkshire. Stephen rushed inside for his camera and managed to take one shot of the light. When it was developed there were three objects on the photograph. Experts examined the negative and declared that they didn't think it had been tampered with. Some people have said it must be a fake because the UFOs are out of focus, whilst the rest of the picture is in focus.

Close encounters

People's reports of UFOs seen at close range are divided into three categories.

1 Close encounters of the first kind
These are simply close sightings of a UFO.

2 Close encounters of the second kind
Similar to first encounters, but in these cases the UFO affects the environment about it. This could mean that grass or trees are flattened or burnt, animals are frightened, electrical equipment is affected, car engines are cut out and headlights are dimmed.

3 Close encounters of the third kind
These are the most dramatic encounters. They involve sighting of, or actual contact with, the occupants of the UFO.

Amazing UFO facts

UFOs have been known as *Flying Saucers* since 1947, when Kenneth Arnold, an American pilot saw several UFOs flying in formation over Washington State in the USA. When he described his encounter with the UFOs, he said that '*They flew like a saucer would if you skipped it across the water*'. The Press took this description and coined the phrase *Flying Saucer* to describe UFOs.

Where are they from?

If UFOs are spacecraft, then they must come from somewhere, but where? Some scientists claim that the nearest star system that could support life is Alpha Centauri. This is so far away that it would take over 100 years to visit earth and return home again, even if the spacecraft travelled faster than we think is possible! Some scientists have countered this by saying that perhaps UFOs are able to travel through time. This would mean that UFOs and their occupants may come from places that we don't even know exist!

Amazing EBE facts

The occupants of UFOs are described by scientists as **Extraterrestrial Biological Entities** (EBEs). Some people claim that up to *nine* different species, or types, of EBEs have visited the earth.

In Steven Spielberg's film *E.T.*, an extraterrestrial creature is stranded on earth after his spaceship flies off without him. He eventually manages to contact his home planet and is rescued. At a special screening of the film at the White House in 1982, Ronald Reagan, the US President of the day, was reported to have whispered to Spielberg that '*There are probably only six people in this room who know how true this is*'.

Has contact been made?

According to some reports, several UFOs have actually crashed on earth and have been recovered along with the occupants.

One such report involves two UFOs colliding and crashing in the State of New Mexico, USA in 1947. Several witnesses described seeing a crashed silver, disc-shaped craft.

What makes this report even more incredible is the fact that the witnesses reported seeing four alien bodies next to the damaged craft. Two of these were supposedly still alive and the witnesses tried to communicate with them.

The disc and the aliens were eventually taken away by soldiers who told the witnesses that they were not allowed to say anything as it was a top secret military aircraft. Those witnesses who have broken silence have stated that it couldn't have been a man-made craft and that the bodies were not human.

The US government deny this incredible story, but why should the witnesses have all made up such a bizarre tale? Is it possible that humans have made contact with beings from other planets?

Mystery monsters

There are hundreds of reports of mysterious creatures that are supposed to live in remote parts of the world. Two of the most famous are *Nessie*, the Loch Ness Monster, and *Bigfoot* – supposedly related to the abominable snowman.

Nessie – Queen of the monsters!

Modern sightings of the Loch Ness Monster go back to 1933, when a local resident saw a 'monster' emerging from the murky depths of Loch Ness in Scotland. Since that day there have been hundreds of sightings, but despite all efforts, no one has yet taken a photograph that without doubt captures Nessie on film.

The first reported sighting of a monster in Loch Ness took place in AD 565. St Columba was on a religious mission in the area when a strange beast attacked one of the travelling party. St Columba commanded the monster not to hurt the man and ordered it to return to the depths. The monster promptly obeyed!

The loch is an ideal home for a mysterious creature to remain undiscovered. Loch Ness is Britain's deepest loch, measuring up to 250 metres deep. It is also 38 km long and 2.5 km wide at its widest point. This massive expanse of fresh water makes it virtually impossible for Nessie hunters to know where the creature may surface next, or where its home may be.

Amazing monster facts

Some people believe that Nessie is a prehistoric creature from the *plesiosaur* family. This explanation seems to fit in with the various descriptions of the creature having humps, flippers and a long tapering neck. However, the flaw in this theory is the fact that plesiosaurs are supposed to have been extinct for 70 million years!

Bigfoot and its cousin!

There are many stories of ape-like creatures that inhabit the wild, lonely places of the world.

In Russia this creature is known as *Alma*, while the people of Tibet know it as a *Yeti* and the Indian tribes of North America give it the name of *Sasquatch*. The mysterious creature is perhaps better known to us as *The Abominable Snowman* or *Bigfoot.*

Sasquatch

The **Sasquatch** supposedly inhabits North America where there have been as many as 1,500 reported sightings over the past 150 years. The creature is described as being anything between 2–3 metres tall and covered in reddish brown hair. It stands on two legs and can travel at great speeds.

The most famous evidence for the existence of the Sasquatch is a cine film recording of one walking into a forest. It was taken in 1967 at Bluff Creek, California by Roger Patterson. The authenticity of the film has been argued about ever since, but if it is a fake, it is a very good one.

The people of the Himalayas believe in the existence of the **Yeti**, a tall, half-human, half-ape-like figure that lives in the mountains.

The Yeti is supposed to be up to 3.6 metres high and covered in thick brown hair.

The only photographic evidence we have of the Yeti is a series of footprints taken by a British climber, Eric Shipton in 1951. Some people have said that the footprints are those of a goat which have melted and consequently look strange. But is it possible for such footprints to look so strange?

Atlantis: The lost world

The story of Atlantis is one of the world's greatest mysteries. Thousands of people have searched for it, but none have ever found it. Some people claim that it never existed and is just a myth.

The story of Atlantis

The Greek philosopher Plato wrote of a wonderful island that lay beyond the Pillars of Hercules.

Atlantis was a huge circular island. Its land was green and fertile and it was rich in precious metals. Because of this, the people of Atlantis were very powerful. They controlled the Mediterranean and developed trading links with many countries.

The capital of Atlantis was defended by five mighty circular walls. Its buildings were splendid and the walls and towers were covered with silver and gold.However, this paradise began to change for the worse. Its people became greedy and corrupt and they planned to take over and rule the world by force.This behaviour was finally punished by the gods who sent volcanic eruptions and tidal waves to destroy Atlantis and its people. In a single day, the whole island sank beneath the sea and Atlantis disappeared from the face of the earth.

Where is Atlantis?

If Atlantis did exist, then where was it located? There have been many theories about where Atlantis may have been. Brazil, Greenland and even Britain have been suggested. However, a recent theory seems to fit in with some of the story told by Plato.

In 1520 BC there was an enormous explosion in the Aegean Sea when the circular-shaped, volcanic island of Thera blew up. It was such a powerful explosion that the island was covered with volcanic ash, in some places over 30 metres thick! Forty years after the explosion, the volcanic cone collapsed and left the island cresent-shaped. The modern day name for Thera is Santorini and many recent archeological finds have provided evidence that a sophisticated civilisation once lived there.

Santorini today

Amazing Atlantian facts

Plato claimed that Atlantis was destroyed 9000 years before the time of Solon who lived around the year 600 BC. Could someone have made an error and added an extra nought to the figure? If this is the case, then the destruction of Atlantis was 900 years before Solon's time. This would give a date of 1500 BC, around the time that Thera was destroyed.

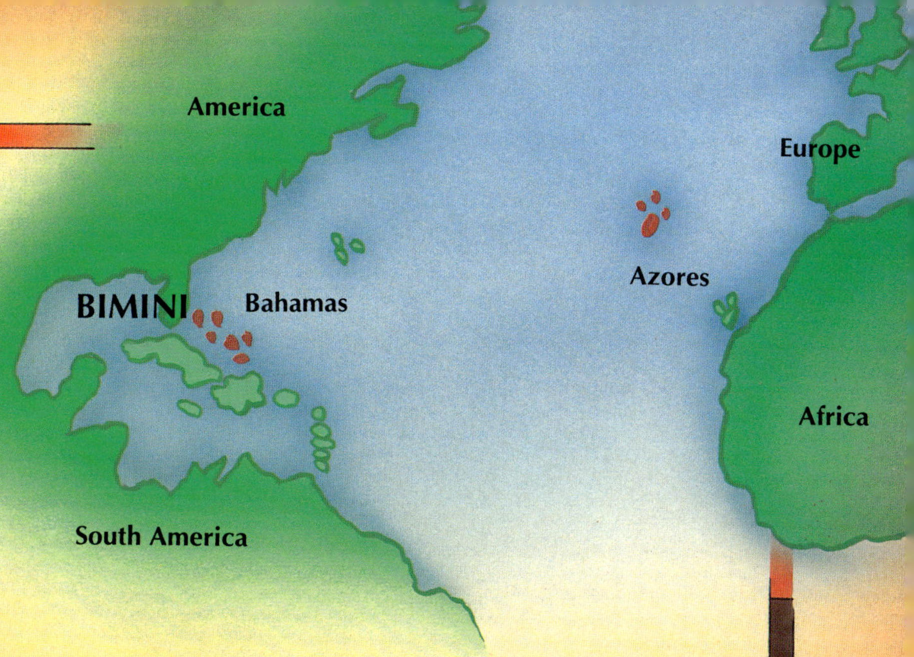

Plato claimed that Atlantis lay beyond the Pillars of Hercules. This was the ancient name for the Strait of Gibraltar. If this is true, it would mean that Atlantis was situated in the Atlantic Ocean. Many people have searched the Atlantic for proof of the island's existence. Some people think that Atlantis was the island of Sao Migual in the Azores. Others claim that the underwater mountains in the middle of the Atlantic Ocean are the remains of the lost world.

More recently attention has switched to an island in the Bahamas. In 1968 airline pilots took photographs of an *underwater city* off the coast of the island of North Bimini. The resulting expeditions found what appeared to be streets, huge stone walls and a marble pillar. Experts are divided as to whether these are man-made or natural formations. More discoveries are helping to support the idea of a lost Atlantic civilisation. Divers have found a flight of stone steps off the coast of Puerto Rico proving that there was some form of civilisation living in this area some 10,000 years ago. Could this have been Atlantis?

Whatever the explanation, the mystery of Atlantis remains and the search for it goes on.

World mystery map

The world is full of mysteries! Some we have already solved, some we think we have solved and some we will never be able to solve!

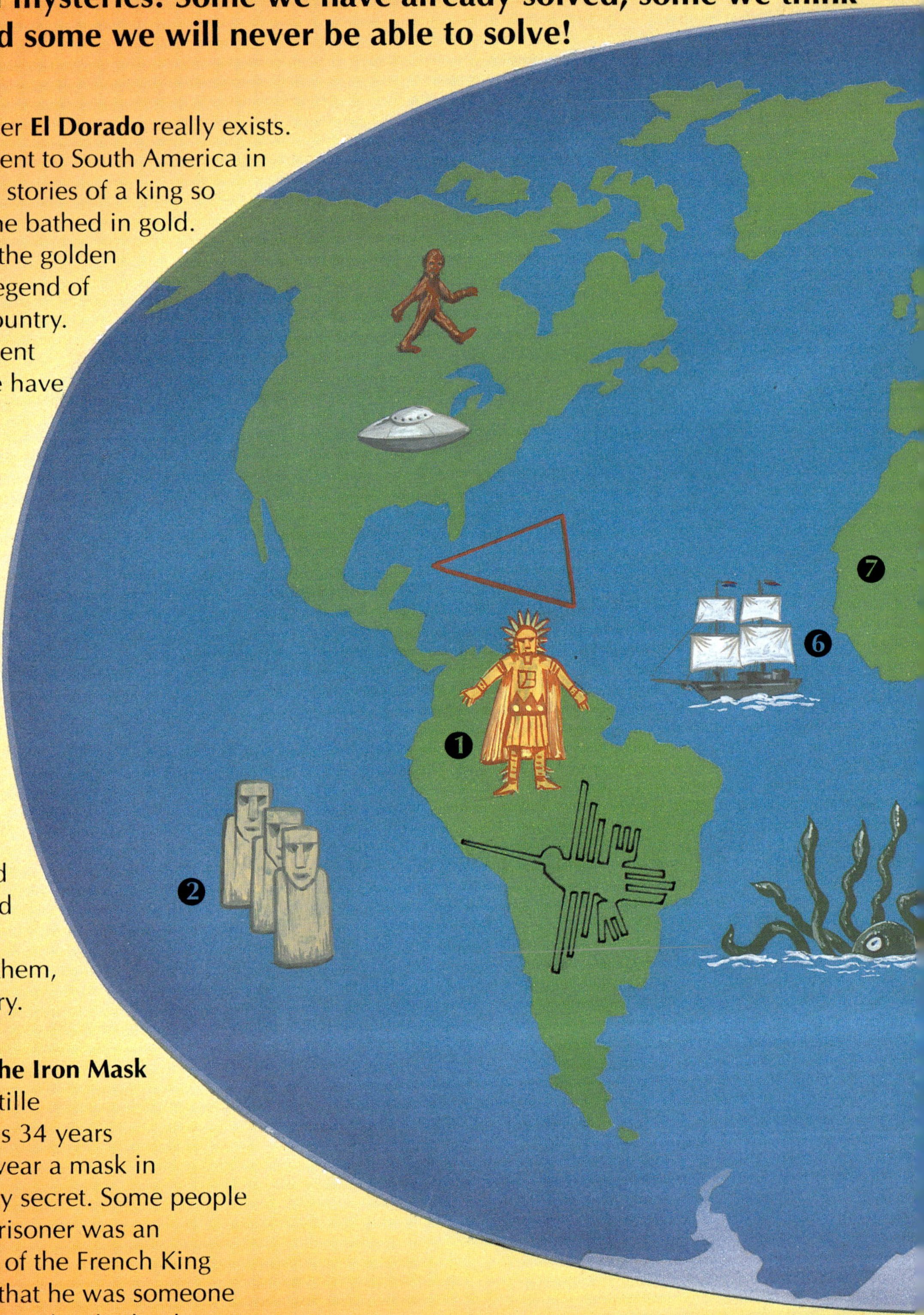

❶ Nobody knows whether **El Dorado** really exists. Spanish conquistadors went to South America in search of gold and heard stories of a king so fabulously wealthy that he bathed in gold. The legend of Eldorado, the golden man, soon became the legend of El Dorado, the golden country. From 1530 until the present day, thousands of people have searched for the lost kingdom of gold, hoping to make their fortunes.

❷ The tall mysterious **Easter Island Statues** are to be found buried, broken or standing on the 116 sq km Easter Island. Some of the statues measure up to 9 m in height and weigh several tonnes. Some experts believe they were made to guard the funeral vaults of dead warriors, but this is only guesswork. Who made them, and why, is still a mystery.

❸ In 1703 **the Man in the Iron Mask** died in the dreaded Bastille in Paris. For the previous 34 years he had been forced to wear a mask in order to keep his identity secret. Some people have claimed that the prisoner was an illegitimate half-brother of the French King Louis XIV, others claim that he was someone who knew a great secret and so had to be locked away.

4 In 1908 there was an **enormous explosion in Siberia**. Because of the remoteness of the explosion site, it was not investigated until 1927. When it was, it was discovered that 200 sq km of forest had been destroyed.

Theories to explain what caused such destruction include: a crashed alien spacecraft, a comet hitting the earth and a black hole striking the planet.

5 Edmund Hillary and Sherpa Tenzing are credited as being the first to climb Mount Everest in 1953, but they may have been beaten to the summit by **George Malory** and **Andrew Irvine.** Malory and Irvine made an assault on Everest's summit in June 1924. They were last seen just below the summit. They never returned and their bodies have never been found, leaving behind the mystery of whether they reached the summit and became the first people to reach the highest point on earth.

6 There have been hundreds of reported sightings of **The Flying Dutchman**, a phantom ship that sails the world's seas with a ghostly crew. The legend of the ship recounts how the Dutch Captain Van der Decken sailed into a storm and defied God to sink the ship. For this blasphemy, the ship and crew were condemned to sail the seas forever.

7 **The Dogon Tribe** in West Africa have a remarkable knowledge about the Universe. They already knew about a star that has only just been discovered. Their knowledge has led people to believe that they must have been visited by alien life-forms in the past.

Mysterious places

There are many mysterious places in the world that defy reasonable explanation.

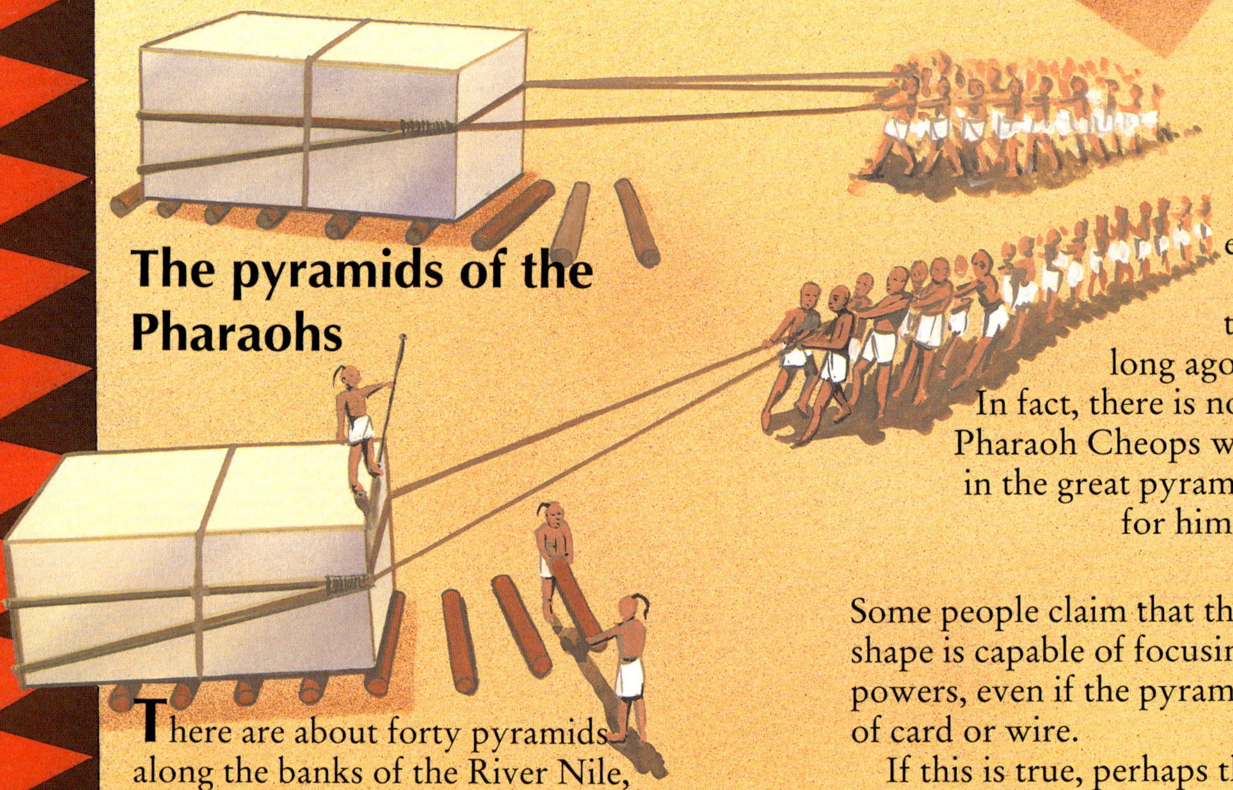

The pyramids of the Pharaohs

There are about forty pyramids along the banks of the River Nile, in Egypt. By far the mightiest are those at Giza – the three pyramids of Chephren, Mycerinus, and the Great Pyramid of Cheops.

The Egyptians believed that when a king died, he went to an after-life and would need his body preserved and his belongings to hand. The bodies of the kings were embalmed, and became **mummies.** The pyramids were their tombs.

The mystery is, what persuaded thousands of people to labour for twenty years or more to create them? If they were meant to guard the body or goods of the dead king, they failed, as no pyramid has ever been found to contain a body – tomb robbers have long ago emptied them all. In fact, there is no evidence that the Pharaoh Cheops was ever laid to rest in the great pyramid his people built for him with such labour!

Some people claim that the pyramid shape is capable of focusing strange powers, even if the pyramid is made of card or wire.

If this is true, perhaps the pyramids were built to preserve the body of the dead king. Whatever the reason, pyramids have the power to awe and amaze us more than forty centuries after they were built.

Amazing pyramid facts

Razor blades kept in a pyramid remain sharp after much use, food remains fresh, and sitting inside a pyramid is said to increase mental power.

The message of the Nazcas

Over a desert plain in Peru are drawn a series of lines. Some are straight and wide like airport runways, while others make up complicated abstract patterns, or pictures of animals or birds. Many mysteries surround these strange pictures. What do they represent? And why, centuries before humans learnt the secret of flight, did the Nazca Indians make huge and complicated patterns that can only be seen from the air?

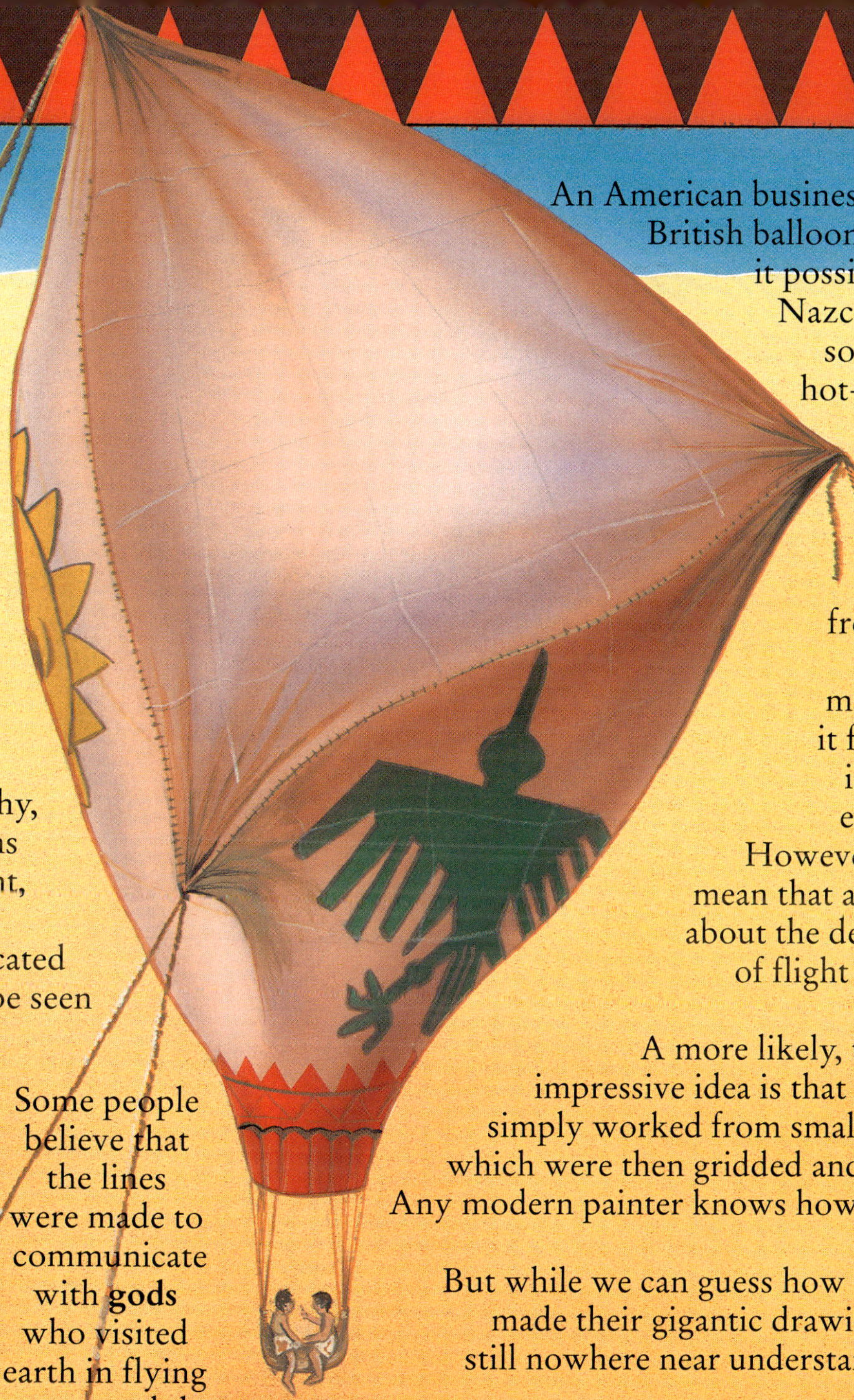

An American businessman and a British balloonist thought it possible that the Nazcas had used some form of hot-air balloon to design the lines. The pair made a balloon from locally-available materials and it flew, so this is a possible explanation. However, it would mean that all our ideas about the development of flight are wrong!

A more likely, though less impressive idea is that the Nazcas simply worked from small drawings, which were then gridded and scaled up. Any modern painter knows how to do this.

But while we can guess how the Nazcas made their gigantic drawings, we are still nowhere near understanding why.

Some people believe that the lines were made to communicate with **gods** who visited earth in flying saucers, and that some of the lines are in fact runways!

Amazing line facts

The Nazca lines are so difficult to see from ground level that the Pan American Highway was built straight through several of them without the builders even noticing that they were there.

The Bermuda Triangle

Strange phenomena have been reported in the area of the Bermuda Triangle since the days of Christopher Columbus.

In December 1945 a flight of Avenger torpedo-bombers left its base at Fort Lauderdale, Florida. The weather was good and the training exercise routine, but after an hour, the Flight Instructor radioed back to base, '*This is an emergency. We seem to be off course. We cannot see land*'. The control tower instructed him to turn to the West . . . '*We don't know which way is West . . . everything is wrong, strange. We aren't sure of any direction. Even the ocean doesn't look as it should . . .*' By now, a storm was brewing. A Mariner seaplane with a crew of 13 was sent out to locate Flight Nineteen. Neither it, nor the five Avengers, returned. The area had claimed more victims, and the phrase **Bermuda Triangle** was coined.

This mysterious area of sea has claimed many victims, from ships disappearing with all hands to aeroplanes which seem to have fallen out of the sky. Sailors and aircraft pilots who have returned from the triangle tell of:

- eerie lights in the sky
- radar echoes showing a huge land mass not shown on any maps
- strange mistbanks
- equipment failure which suddenly corrects itself.

Speculations as to the cause of these effects vary from underwater volcanoes through black holes to the favourite standby, UFOs (in Steven Spielberg's film *Close Encounters*, the aircrew of Flight Nineteen are returned to earth by friendly aliens) . . .

Many people are firmly convinced that there is something mysterious and deadly about the Triangle, but others point out that:

- the area is a busy one, where sudden changes in the weather are common
- many inexperienced sailors and pilots do not prepare themselves properly for the tricky condition of the Triangle
- there is little evidence that some of the strange events (such as the Eastern Airlines plane that disappeared off radar screens for ten minutes, then reappeared with every clock and watch on board running ten minutes slow) ever really happened at all!

As it seems impossible to prove whether the losses in the Triangle are due to natural causes (such as storms) or unknown forces, it is likely that the legend of the Bermuda Triangle will last for as long as people take to the sea, or air, and fail to return.

Amazing Triangle facts

The Japanese freighter *Raifuku Maru* disappeared in The Bermuda Triangle in 1925 after sending the message '*Now very danger – come quick*'! A victim of strange forces in the Triangle?

The Mary Celeste: A jinxed ship?

The disappearance of the crew of the *Mary Celeste* remains one of the great mysteries of the sea, one that will probably never be solved.

On 5 December 1872, the crew of a British sailing ship, the *Dei Gratia*, sighted a ship that appeared to be in trouble. Captain David Morehouse of the *Dei Gratia* ordered three of his men to board it to investigate. They rowed across, climbed on board and searched the ship from stem to stern. They found no one. The crew had disappeared completely. The name of the ghost-like ship was the *Mary Celeste.*

Although there was some damage to the *Mary Celeste,* it was in good enough condition to sail and there were ample provisions on board. On closer inspection, it was discovered that a lifeboat and the navigation instruments were missing. It appeared that the crew had abandoned ship. But why?

The *Mary Celeste* had set sail from New York on 7 November 1872 with a cargo of crude alcohol bound for Genoa, Italy. The master of the ship was the 37-year-old Benjamin Spooner Briggs, an experienced sea captain. He was accompanied by his wife, Sarah, their two-year-old daughter, Sophia and a crew of seven men.

For three weeks there was fine weather and the *Mary Celeste* made good progress. However, after the ship had sailed past the Azores, the weather got worse, with moderate gales blowing, but not bad enough to force the crew to abandon a perfectly seaworthy ship for the dangers of a small lifeboat.

The crew of the *Dei Gratia* discovered a log book in Captain Briggs' cabin. The last entry in the log of the *Mary Celeste* was dated 25 November and gave the position of the ship. There were no other clues as to the fate of the captain and crew.

The *Mary Celeste* was brought into Gibraltar on 12 December by three crew members of the *Dei Gratia.* There was an immediate enquiry, where many wild theories were put forward to explain the crew's disappearance. Nothing was decided and Morehouse and his crew were awarded a salvage fee of £1700. A new crew and captain took over the *Mary Celeste* and the ship sailed on to deliver her goods in Genoa.

Several theories have been put forward to explain the disappearance of the crew.

One of the earliest stories accused the captains of the two ships of plotting together in order to claim the salvage. This story said that Captain Briggs of the *Mary Celeste* killed his crew and then took to the lifeboat to meet up with Captain Morehouse at some pre-arranged destination. There is no evidence to back this theory up, and it fails to take into account the fact that Briggs was a part owner of the *Mary Celeste.*

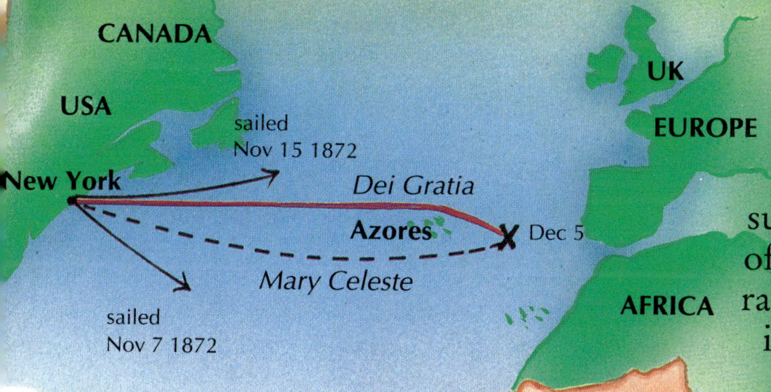

There was also the suggestion that the crew of the *Dei Gratia* killed the crew of the *Mary Celeste* in order to get their cargo. However, a Vice Admiralty Court, cleared the crew of the *Dei Gratia* of any suspicion. Another claim was that the crew of the *Mary Celeste* had gone on a drunken rampage. This theory was discredited when it was pointed out that the type of alcohol being carried by the *Mary Celeste* would probably kill anyone drinking it.

More incredible theories include waterspouts and whirlwinds that sucked up the crew, sea monsters that ate everyone on board and alien beings in UFOs who abducted the crew and took them back to another planet!

Amazing mystery facts

The Mary Celeste was originally called The Amazon. It ran aground on its first voyage and afterwards regularly ran aground and collided with other ships!

Powers of stone

Stonehenge, on Salisbury Plain, is one of the great mysteries of the British Isles. Nobody knows exactly how it was built, or why.

Stone circles

According to legend, the stones were brought from Ireland by Merlin. Modern studies have concluded that most of the stones were quarried locally, though some were brought from as far away as Wales. There are many theories about what the stones might have been:

- the remains of a temple of the druids
- a great stone calendar
- an energy transmitter or a beacon for UFOs
- an ancient racecourse or bullring
- a war memorial or royal tomb.

None of these claims has ever been proved conclusively.

It has been suggested that Stonehenge was a gigantic **astronomical clock.** Some of the stones point to the position of the sunrise on Midsummer's day, and others seem to point to other significant positions of the sun and moon throughout the year. However, in other stone circles there are no significant astronomical alignments at all. There seems to be no way of guessing at the true purposes behind the building of the magnificent circles.

Standing stones

Standing Stones known as **megaliths** can be found all over the world. Not all are set in circles. Some stand alone, like the eight metre high pillar in the churchyard at Rudston, Humberside. Others stand in small groups like the Devil's Arrows in Yorkshire.

The petrified army

In Brittany, standing stones are called **menhirs.** Some 3,000 of these are set out in lines at Carnac. According to local legend, the stones are a petrified army of pagan warriors turned to stone by Pope Cornelius. Such menhirs, singly and in groups, are common in northern France. Sometimes one stone is laid across several standing stones to act as a kind of table – this is called a **dolmen.**

Carnac

Nobody knows why our ancestors built these monuments or why they suddenly stopped. We can only marvel at those that remain and wonder why our ancestors – in Europe, Mexico, India, North America, Africa, even China and Japan – carved and erected these great stones centuries ago. This is perhaps the only example in human history of all peoples working with a common purpose, though we can no longer guess what that purpose may have been.

Strange powers

There are five commonly recognised senses – touch, taste, sight, smell and hearing – which we use to find things out. Could there be others?

Although it is very difficult to prove, it seems that some people, called **clairvoyants**, have special powers of the mind known as **ESP – Extrasensory Perception.**

Prophecy is the ability to describe things that have not yet happened.

The most famous prophet of all was **Nostrodamus.** Though he died in 1566, his followers claim that he accurately predicted the landing of men on the moon. However, others say that his prophecies are so vague that they can be made to mean anything.

We should hope that Nostrodamus was not an accurate prophet, as he forecast the end of the world in 1999.

Using a Y-shaped stick or pendulum, **dowsers** can locate underground water or minerals or lines of 'earthforce'. The stick or pendulum is held in the dowser's hands and twitches or bends when a possible spot is found.

In the 1960s, Tom Lethbridge, a retired archaeologist, claimed to be able to tell by the rate of swing and length of his dowsing pendulum exactly what substance was buried.

Dowsing can be taught, but the student must have some talent to begin with.

Precognition is a glimpse of a single future event, such as a disaster. In 1898 a book written by Morgan Robertson was published in which a huge ocean liner, the *Titan* hits an iceberg in the Atlantic and sinks. It was published fourteen years before the *Titanic* went down in exactly the way described in the book. Did the author catch a glimpse of the future?

Amazing levitating facts

The French explorer Alexandra David-Neel met a holy man in Tibet who had practised levitation to such an extent that he had to be bound in chains to prevent him floating away!

Telepathy is the supposed ability to communicate with another person mind-to-mind. It is difficult to prove that this ability exists.

However in 1930, the well-known writer Upton Sinclair published a book, *Mental Radio*, which described how he and others had 'transmitted' pictures to his wife, Mary Craig, with an outstanding degree of accuracy. The preface to the book was written by one of the greatest scientists of all time, Albert Einstein.

Some people claim to be able to tell when something is disturbing a person with whom they are very close, especially in times of danger. This ability, which seems to be most common between twins, is called **empathy.**

Levitation is the act of lifting one's body from the ground by the power of the mind alone. It is mostly associated with the mystics and holy men of the East.

Telekinesis (or **Psychokinesis**) is the ability to move an object with the power of mind alone.

Harry Price, who also investigated Borley Rectory (see **Ghosts**), observed a young woman called Stella Cranshaw move and play small musical instruments which were locked in a double cage.

Is it possible for the mind to have power over physical objects? In the 1970s, **Uri Geller** demonstrated on television that he could bend metal objects such as spoons by gently rubbing them. Viewers rang with claims that cutlery had bent in their own homes during Geller's broadcast.

Many people suspected a hoax, but nobody has yet explained how he produced the effect.

The death of the dinosaurs

Why did the great reptiles of prehistoric times suddenly disappear from the face of the planet?

Dinosaurs dominated the earth for nearly 150 million years, from the Triassic to the Cretaceous periods. Some dinosaurs were no bigger than a chicken, others like the **Diplodocus** could grow up to 27 metres long and weigh nearly 30 tonnes.

Suddenly, about sixty-five million years ago, the dinosaurs disappeared and became extinct. This disappearance didn't take place overnight, but over a period of a few thousand years. However, compared to the time they had existed on the planet, their death was sudden and mysterious. What happened to the dinosaurs?

Why did they die?

There are several theories which try to explain why dinosaurs became extinct, and there is a great deal of work being undertaken by scientists to support these theories.

Some scientists believe that the mass-extinction was caused by a star in a nearby constellation exploding. Supposedly this would have caused the earth's surface to be covered by deadly cosmic rays which led to the death of the dinosaurs. However, this theory has two flaws. Firstly, there is no evidence that such an explosion ever took place and secondly, it doesn't explain why only some creatures were killed off.
If the rays did cover the earth's surface why weren't all living creatures destroyed?

Another theory that is becoming increasingly popular with scientists is the *meteorite theory* - the idea that the earth was hit by a giant meteorite measuring up to 15 km wide! This theory is based on the fact that scientists have discovered large traces of a metal called iridium, which is only found in large amounts in meteorites, asteroids and comets.

Another popular theory is based on a gradual change in the earth's climate. Evidence has been found that the earth's climate became cooler. Dinosaurs, being cold-blooded creatures, could not adapt to the new conditions and as the plants they fed on died out they either froze to death or starved. There is much work being undertaken to try and prove this climate change theory, but the chances of our ever being able to fully solve the mystery of the death of the dinosaurs are still very slim.

Amazing dinosaur facts

In 1841 Sir Richard Owen made up the word 'dinosaur' from two Greek words 'Deinos' and 'Souros', which mean 'Terrible Lizard'.

The curse of Tutankhamun

To protect the tombs of the dead from being robbed, the Ancient Egyptians put warnings on the tombs, pronouncing that anyone who stole or desecrated the burial chambers would be cursed.

The beginnings of the curse?

In 1922, the English archaeologists Lord Carnarvon and Howard Carter discovered the tomb of the boy-pharaoh, Tutankhamun, in the Valley of the Kings at Luxor. The tomb contained the mummified body of the king and a hoard of priceless treasure.

Before the archeologists entered the tomb, they found a stone tablet with a curse written in hieroglyphics. It warned that: '*Death will slay with its wings whoever disturbs the pharaoh's peace*'. Carter and Carnarvon ignored this and opened the tomb. But did this action bring down on their heads the curse of Tutankhamun?

Lord Carnarvon

Victims of the curse?

The first victim of the curse was Carter's pet canary, which the Egyptian workers believed would bring them luck. Soon after the tomb was opened, the canary was eaten by a cobra. Egyptians believed that this snake was the earthly form of the goddess Wadjet, the protector of Egyptian royalty.

At the same time, Lord Carnarvon's health began to deteriorate. He suffered raging fever and in his delirious state could be heard to mutter '*A bird is scratching at my face*'. It was another Egyptian belief that the Nekhebet bird would scratch the face of anyone violating a pharaoh's tomb. Two months after entering the tomb, Carnarvon died. As he took his last breath, all the lights in Cairo went out for five minutes!

The curse seemed to claim the lives of several people.

- George Jay-Gould an American multi-millionaire contracted a fever on the very same day he visited the tomb, and died shortly after.
- Professor La Fleur died on the night he entered the tomb.
- Joel Woolf, a British industrialist, one of the first visitors to see the tomb fell into a coma and died on the way back to Britain.
- A.C. Mace and Richard Bethell died within a few years of the discovery – they had been Carter's assistants.

The curse continues?

In 1966 it was decided to arrange an exhibition of Tutankhamun's treasure in Paris. The director of Egyptian Antiquities, who was dealing with the proposed exhibition, dreamt that there would be danger if the treasures left Egypt. Following a meeting to finalise arrangements, he was knocked down and killed by a car.

His successor, Dr Gamal Mehrez, refused to believe in a curse and went ahead with organising a foreign exhibition. He gave permission for the treasures to be shipped to London in 1972. As the mask of Tutankhamun was taken to the airport, Dr Mehrez dropped down dead.

Howard Carter

Amazing Tutankhamun facts

By 1929, seven years after the opening of the tomb, twenty-two people who had been involved with Tutankhamun's tomb had died. Only two of the original excavators were still alive. One of these was Howard Carter. He finally died in 1939 without any apparent ill effects from the curse.

Coincidence or curse?

Mysteries feed on coincidences. Perhaps it was just coincidence that the people involved with the discovery died soon after. Strange things do happen after all.

Some people have tried to explain the mystery in scientific terms. It has been suggested that the Egyptians coated the tombs with poisons or even radio-active rocks. Another suggestion to explain the deaths of the excavators is that a form of bacteria was present in the tomb which infected some of the visitors and workers.

The man who put this idea forward was killed in a car crash shortly afterwards! But for many people the explanation is a simple one – the *Curse of Tutankhamun* is real.

Index

ISBN 1-86019-542-3
First published 1993

This edition published 1997 by Brockhampton Press, a member of Hodder Headline PLC Group.

10 9 8 7 6 5 4 3 2 1
1999 1998 1997

Typeset by Litho Link Ltd, Welshpool, Powys, Wales.
Printed in India.
A CIP record is registered by and held at the British Library.

Acknowledgements

The authors and Publishers would like to thank the following for their permission to reproduce copyright photographs in this book: Amblin Entertainment/MCA Publishing Rights, a division of MCA Inc. - p.8; Janet & Colin Bord - pp24, 25; Mary Evans Picture Library - pp4, 5, 6, 23; Fortean Picture Library - pp6, 10, 11; Robert Harding Picture Library - p14; Hulton Deutsch Collection - pp30, 31; Royal Geographical Society - p11; Strathmore Estates - p4; Topham Picture Library - p27.

Cover illustration by Barry Jones.